A BEACON BIOGRAPHY

GAL GADOT

Tamra B. Orr

PURPLE TOAD
PUBLISHING

PURPLE TOAD
PUBLISHING

Printing   1   2   3   4   5   6   7   8   9

A Beacon Biography

Publisher's Cataloging-in-Publication Data
Orr, Tamra B.
  Gal Gadot / written by Tamra B. Orr.
    p. cm.
Includes bibliographic references, glossary, and index.
ISBN 9781624693892
1. Gadot, Gal, 1985-. 2. Actresses--Israel--Biography--Juvenile literature. I. Series: Beacon biography.
 PN2287 2017
 791.43092

Library of Congress Control Number: 2017956828

eBook ISBN: 9781624693908

ABOUT THE AUTHOR: Tamra B. Orr is a full-time author living in the Pacific Northwest with her family. She graduated from Ball State University in Muncie, Indiana. She has written more than 500 books about everything from historical events and career choices to controversial issues and celebrity biographies. On those rare occasions that she is not writing a book, she is reading one. She makes sure to keep up on all superhero movies and admits *Wonder Woman* is her current favorite.

PUBLISHER'S NOTE: This story has not been authorized or endorsed by Gal Gadot.

CONTENTS

This future Wonder Woman's smile helped her become the superstar she is today.

NOT
Miss Universe

When 18-year-old Gal Gadot (*GALL gah-DOHT*) heard her name announced as Miss Israel in the 2004 beauty pageant, she could not believe it. She had just graduated from high school and had only joined the beauty competition because her mother suggested it and sent in her photograph. She was far more into sports and being outside than putting on fancy dresses and makeup. "I'm just not that type of girl," she told Jimmy Kimmel in 2016 on his television late-night show. When she won, she wasn't thrilled. In fact, she was scared.

Gadot did not want to keep being in these contests. It was a bit overwhelming. "I was like, 'What? Miss Israel? All the responsibility of being Miss Israel?' " she told *W Magazine*. As Miss Israel, she would travel to schools, visit other countries, and raise money for charities. She would also automatically be entered in the upcoming Miss Universe pageant—another thing she did not want to do. "I thought it'd

Gadot's gowns helped her win—even when she wore ones to try to lose!

be cool to tell my grandkids that grandma was in the Miss Israel pageant," she admitted to *Glamour* magazine. "I never thought I'd win. And when I won, it freaked me out so much I did everything in my powers during Miss Universe that they didn't pick me." To *W Magazine,* Gadot admitted she misbehaved as much as possible so that she would not win. "I'm a really good girl but because I was afraid I would win again . . . I came late in all the rehearsals and I wasn't wearing the right evening gowns."

Losing the Miss Universe pageant was not disappointing for Gadot. It was exactly what she wanted. She had other plans for her life, and none of them included evening gowns or bikinis. Instead, they included military training and then college. Little did she know that one day, her face would be known all over the world, and not just for being Miss Israel. One day she would be known across the planet as the one and only Wonder Woman.

Gadot had little idea of her exciting future.

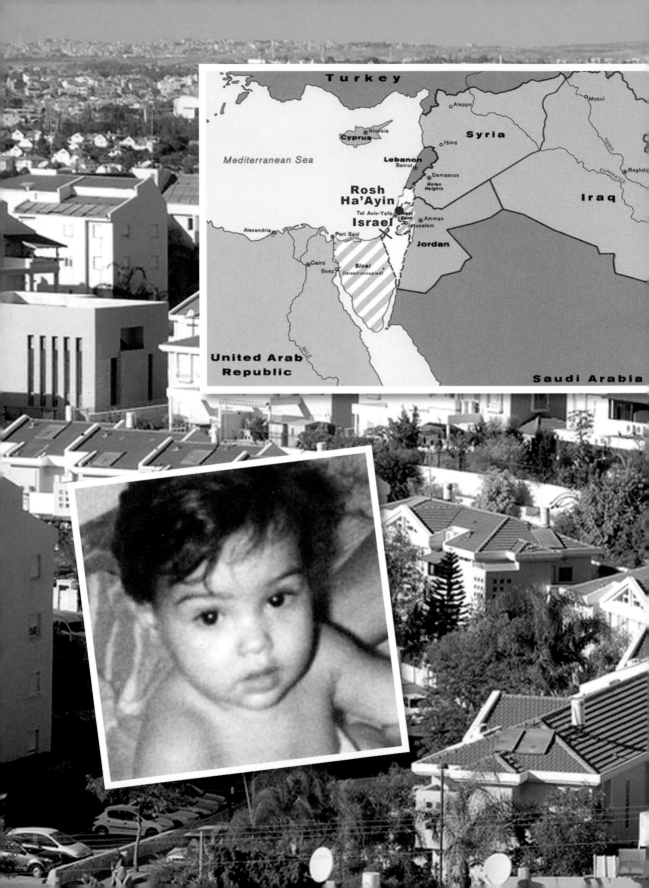

Gal Gadot was born in a busy city in the country of Israel.

"Look at Me!"

Gal was born on April 30, 1985, in Rosh Ha'Ayin, Israel, to Michael and Init Gadot. It only took her a couple of years to realize she enjoyed being the center of attention. "I don't remember this," she told *Vanity Fair*, "but my mom told me that when I was three, they threw a party on the rooftop of the house. They put me to bed, and I heard people coming into the house and no one came to me. I went to the rooftop and took a hose and I started to spray water on everyone, just to get attention." According to an interview on *NME*, the little girl then cried out, "It's meeee! Look at meeeeee!" As Gadot added in her *Glamour* interview, "Very elegant, right? I loved the attention. But I never connected all the dots that maybe I should be an actress."

Gadot's mother was a physical education teacher who strongly believed in the importance of fresh air, sunshine, and exercise for Gal and her younger sister, Dana. Far more time was spent outside exploring than inside watching television. "My mom is amazing," Gadot told ESPN reporter Allison Glock. "Because of her, I was so

Gadot spent most of her time in motion, either in her backyard or on a dance floor.

active my entire life. There was no TV time. There was, 'take the ball and go outside and play with the neighbors.' "

Instead of television, the family often enjoyed watching movies together. "In the evening after having dinner, we used to sit down and watch movies," Gadot told *Bring the Noise*, "and on the weekends, they used to take my sister and me to the theater. So I always had the passion but I was not aware of it."

For many years, Gadot focused on learning all kinds of dance. "I was a dancer for 12 years—ballet, hip-hop, modern, jazz," she told *Vanity Fair*. "I thought that I wanted to be a choreographer." In addition to dance, Gadot played a number of sports, including tennis, basketball, and volleyball. She considered herself a tomboy. When she was given a journal at the age of 12, Gadot told *Marie Claire*, "I tried writing in it because my friends did. I felt like I was faking it. *Hi, dear diary* . . . Like, who is going to care?"

When *Glamour* asked Gadot who her real-life "wonder woman" was, she did not hesitate to answer. "My mum, she just gave my sister and me really good, strong inner confidence and she gave us the ability to believe in ourselves and aspire to our dreams."

While Gadot was a teenager at Begin High School in Rosh Ha'Ayin, she began getting offers to model. She had very little interest. After graduation, she was sure she wanted to go in another direction—the military. In Israel, all young people must serve two years in the Israel Defense Forces, learning weapons and combat training. It is a tradition,

Time in Israel's army taught Gadot many lessons about being strong and fit.

and most of the people living there accept it as part of being a citizen. "Part of being Israeli is to go to the army," Gadot explained to *People*. "All my friends went, my parents went, and my grandparents went."

Serving in the military is not easy, of course. "You give two or three years, and it's not about you," Gadot told *NME*. "You give your freedom away. You learn discipline and respect." As she told *Marie Claire* in 2015, "To become a fight-training instructor in the Israel Defense Forces, I did a four-month boot camp where I had to go for seven-mile runs every morning at 6:30 a.m. It was good prep for acting," she added, "because movies require a lot of discipline and responsibility."

Once her time in the army was over, it was off to college. She planned to major in law and international relations, and enrolled at Reichman Law School at the Interdisciplinary Center in the city of Herzliya. While there, a casting director saw her modeling card on an agency bulletin board. He called her and asked her to be a Bond girl.

Although Gadot was a successful model, it was only one step on her way to stardom on the screen.

Law School versus Bond Girl

Gal Gadot knew what she wanted: to be a lawyer. Modeling and acting jobs kept coming her way, but she knew that she was too focused to be distracted by acting. That changed when the casting director called her to see if Gadot would be interested in playing a character named Camille Montes in the new James Bond film, *Quantum of Solace*.

"I told him, 'No way!' " Gadot told *W Magazine*. "I said, 'I'm studying law and international relations. I'm way too serious and smart to be an actress, and besides, the script is all in English.' I spoke English, but I wasn't comfortable with it."

Once she stopped worrying, Gadot decided to try out for the part. She promptly lost it to Ukrainian actor Olga Kurylenko. "It was always Olga's," Gadot told *Glamour*.

Even though she did not get the role, the chance of getting it was enough to renew Gadot's interest in acting. To improve her skills, she hired an acting coach and dropped out of college. In 2007, she was hired to star in one season of the Israeli television series *Bubot* (Babes).

The cast of *Bubot* helped make the show a hit on Iraeli television.

The show was about mysteries and crimes happening in the modeling world. Gadot played a character named Miriam Elkayam.

After being on television, Gadot knew that she wanted to continue acting. Fortunately, she was offered one of the best roles she could have imagined. In 2009, she was hired to play weapons expert Gisele Yashar in the fourth *Fast & Furious* movie. She absolutely loved the character.

"Today it is very rare to see tough women on screen," she explained to *Real Style Network*. "Usually the woman is saved and rescued by the man. Gisele is very feminine, soft, and intelligent, yet she is strong and independent. . . . That's why I love Gisele. She's a real woman, her character reflects reality nowadays where women need to have it all. . . . [They] need to be strong, smart, and independent."

The character of Gisele Yashar continued into *Fast 5* in 2011, *Fast & Furious 6* in 2013, and even *Furious 7* in 2015. In each film, Gadot did the almost unthinkable—she did all of her own stunts, including jumping off a motorcycle onto a Jeep, and fighting between two cars. "The adrenaline was just incredible and I enjoyed being able to do the stuff that in real life you can't," Gadot confessed to *Real Style Network*. Her years as a tomboy and in the military helped make her strong and gutsy. "I want to have gunshots, I want to fly up in the air, on the

Fast & Furious cast members (left to right): Dwayne Johnson, Gal Gadot, Jordana Brewster, Vin Diesel, and Paul Walker.

motorcycle, whatever," she stated. "I want to do it all myself—no stuntwoman." The stunt coordinators were in charge of making sure Gadot, as well as the rest of the cast, did everything safely. "We were working with [stunt coordinators] for weeks and weeks before we were ready to shoot the scenes," Gadot told *Bring the Noise*. "It was amazing because I felt so safe while I was doing such crazy stuff because I knew they had my back."

Even though she was often covered in bruises after making the Fast & Furious movies, Gadot was thrilled to keep being cast in the films. She had become close friends with everyone in the cast, and Gadot described each film she did as "like a family reunion—coming back home."

Gadot and movie costar Vin Diesel became close friends during their films together.

Gadot's movie roles often sent her to exotic locations, such as Kathmandu in Nepal.

Gadot's acting career was going well. In addition to her repeated role as Gisele, she also had roles in the movies *Knight and Day* and *Date Night*. In 2011, she starred in a television miniseries called *Kathmandu*. She auditioned for the role of Nebula in the film *Guardians of the Galaxy*, but ultimately the job went to Scottish actor Karen Gillan.

Stardom had not arrived yet—but it was about to, thanks to a couple of caped superheroes.

Gadot often appears on panels at comic book conventions. "I just keep active—everything that's challenging me, everything that I feel like doing," she said.

Stardom—and Motherhood

While the world was getting to know Gadot as the Fast & Furious movie chain's Gisele, she was getting to know a businessman and real estate developer from Holland named Yaron Versano. They first met at a party in the Israel desert in 2006. "It was all about yoga, chakras, and eating healthy," Gadot recalled to *Glamour*. "We didn't exactly find ourselves there, but we found each other."

Versano knew immediately that she was *the one*. "I was too young to get it," Gadot continued. "He did! He's ten years older than me. He told me on our second date he was serious and wasn't going to wait more than two years to ask me to marry him. Fast-forward two years: he proposed," she added with a grin. The two were married in 2008. From that day on, Versano has continued to be Gadot's number one fan. As she told *Glamour*, "I wouldn't be able to do what I do without him."

In 2011, Gadot and her husband welcomed their first child, a daughter named Alma. Gadot's filming schedule required her to do a great deal of traveling. Like many new mothers, she felt bad about moving her young daughter from one location to the next. In the *Glamour* interview, she said that her husband gave her some helpful

At home, Gadot shows Alma how to light the candles for Shabbat, the weekly Jewish day of rest.

advice. "When Alma was around two, I was truly anxious about how to travel with a child, moving her from one country to the other, all the different languages," she stated. "It was my husband who told me, 'Gal, think about what kind of role model you want to be. If you want to show Alma that she can follow her dreams, that's what you should do, and we will figure out the logistics.'"

At one point, Gadot thought about giving up acting. She had enjoyed being in films, but she was not sure she was ever going to get a leading role. When director Zack Snyder called her and asked her to come in and audition for him, she thought she would give it one more try. "They wouldn't say what [the role was]," she explained to Ellen DeGeneres on the *Ellen* show. "It was just super confidential."

Half a dozen young actors showed up for the audition, each one taking a turn. Waiting was awful for Gadot. "Waiting is my enemy Number One," she told *W Magazine*. "I was losing my mind. So, I decided to put on Beyoncé . . . 'Who Runs the World? Girls!' I just started to dance, and I let my anxiety go. Thank you, Beyoncé."

Gadot read a scene with Snyder and it went very well. Later, she had a camera test with actor Ben Affleck. Finally, after two weeks, Snyder called her back to let her know the role was for no one other than Wonder Woman in the upcoming DC Comics movie *Batman v. Superman: Dawn of Justic*e.

"Zack called me and he was saying, 'Well, I'm not sure if you have it in Israel, but did you ever hear about Wonder Woman?' I think I went dead for a few good seconds, came back to life, and then tried to pull off my coolest voice, saying, 'Wonder Woman, yeah, of course,'" Gadot told Ellen.

A few weeks later, after flying back to the United States, Gadot saw she had missed 30 calls from her agent. Without getting off the landed plane, she called him back. She was quickly told that she could not tell anyone, but she had gotten the part. Gadot said she screamed. "Everyone [on the plane] looked at me and I couldn't say anything," she told Ellen.

Soon the rest of the world would find out what Gadot now knew: she was going to be Wonder Woman.

Justice League actors (left to right): Ben Affleck (Batman), Ezra Miller (the Flash), Gal Gadot (Wonder Woman), Ray Fisher (Cyborg), and Jason Momoa (Aquaman).

The Wonderful Wonder Woman

If you have not read the history behind the character of Wonder Woman, it helps to know what her mission on Earth is. Legend states that the warrior was first sculpted from clay and brought to life by the Greek god Zeus. She was raised by the Amazons, a group of warrior women who live separately from men. In the comics, she is dedicated to fighting for love and justice. She has the help of magical bracelets, a shield, and a rope (or lasso) to help her conquer evil.

Gadot was thrilled to be cast in this warrior role. In an interview with *NME*, she said, "It's a huge honor to be the one who got this amazing opportunity to tell such an important story. I have a four-year-old daughter and she adores princesses. At the same time, she would tell me, 'The princess, she's so weak; she falls asleep, the prince will come and save her and kiss her and he's the hero.' So I'm so happy to be the one that's going to tell Wonder Woman's story."

She continued, "It's such an important story to tell and I'm grateful for it, but I also think that it's so important for girls and boys to have a strong female superhero to look up to. . . . I'm very, very happy to be a part of that."

Some fans were not pleased about the choice of Gadot for the role. They did not think she was tall enough (she is 5 feet 10 inches), muscular enough, or even curvy enough. "You can't please them all," she told *NME*, "and for me, being an actress, my responsibility is not to pay too much attention to all the noise around me but to pay attention to the script, to the director . . . and protect the character and try to tell her story the best I can. I can only do my best." To train for the film and

build up her muscle mass, she took classes in a variety of martial arts, including kung fu, kickboxing, and jujitsu.

While fans may have had their doubts about Gadot as Wonder Woman, once she appeared in the movie, she was a huge hit. She was immediately hired not only to get her own movie, but also to star in a Justice League film.

Gadot kindly welcomes fans' questions and comments when she appears at comic cons and other events.

Director Patty Jenkins (left) is used to bringing out the best in her actresses. She directed her Monster *star Charlize Theron to an Academy Award for Best Actress.*

As if the physical role of Wonder Woman was not enough, Gadot had another challenge: she was pregnant during much of the filming of the movie. The director of *Wonder Woman*, Patty Jenkins, was amazed by what Gadot was still able to do. She told *EW*, "She's pregnant during part of the movie, in a suit out in a field in the freezing cold. . . . There are so many things we asked her to do. . . . Every day it was a hilarious gauntlet and she would do it."

Gadot said it was not easy. In November 2016 while doing reshoots, she had to wear a green screen on her belly. "On close-up, I looked very much like Wonder Woman," Gadot admitted to *EW*. "On wide shots, I looked very funny, like Wonder Woman pregnant with Kermit the Frog." In the spring of 2017, daughter Maya was born.

In the first two months after its release in June 2017, *Wonder Woman* grossed more than $700 million. It out-earned similar films, including *Spiderman: Homecoming* and *Guardians of the Galaxy*, and it has received great reviews. Gadot told *Glamour*, "When I saw myself in the mirror wearing the Wonder Woman costume for the first time, I was like, 'Oh my God. Who would have thought me, Gal, from this tiny part of the world, would be here in *this* room in the States in *this* role?" Gadot will be returning in that costume and in that role for at least two more films. There is little doubt that she will keep being a wonder-ful woman.

Gadot wore a glittery dress and a big smile at the premiere of Wonder Woman.

1985   Gal Gadot is born on April 30 in Rosh Ha'Ayin, Israel.

School years She takes dance lessons in ballet, hip-hop, modern, and jazz; she plays tennis, basketball, and volleyball. She graduates from Begin High School in Rosh Ha'Ayin.

2004   She is named Miss Israel.

2005   She joins the Israel Defense Forces and becomes a fight-training instructor. After her commitment, she begins college at Reichman Law School and Interdisciplinary Center in the city of Herzliya, Israel. A casting director asks her to audition for the part of Camille Montes in the James Bond film *Quantum of Solace*. She does not get the role.

2006   She meets businessman Yaron Versano at a party in Israel.

2007   Gadot leaves law school and hires an acting coach. She stars in an Israeli television series called *Bubot* (Babes).

2008   Gadot and Yaron Versano marry.

2009   Gadot plays Gisele Yashar in *Fast & Furious*, the fourth movie in the Fast & Furious franchise.

2011   Her daughter, Alma, is born.

2016   She lands the role of Wonder Woman in *Batman v. Superman: Dawn of Justice*.

2017   Her second daughter, Maya, is born. The movie *Wonder Woman* is released to rave reviews.

FILMOGRAPHY

2018	**Justice League: Part Two**
2017	*Wonder Woman; Justice League*
2016	*Batman v. Superman: Dawn of Justice; Criminal; Keeping Up with the Joneses; Triple 9*
2015	*Furious 7*
2013	*Fast & Furious 6*
2011	*Fast 5; Kathmandu*
2010	*Date Night; Knight and Day*
2009	*Fast & Furious*
2007–2008	*Bubot* **(Israeli television series)**

Books

Fridolfs, Derek. *Fort Solitude*. New York: Scholastic, 2016.

Korte, Steve. *Wonder Woman: I Am an Amazon Warrior*. New York: HarperCollins, 2017.

Korte, Steve. *Wonder Woman: The Junior Novel*. New York: HarperFestival, 2017.

Sherman, Jill. *Gal Gadot: Soldier, Model, Wonder Woman*. Minneapolis: Lerner Publications, 2018.

Works Consulted

Bayley, Leanne. "Gal Gadot: The Woman We'll ALL Be Talking about in June." *Glamour Magazine*, May 30, 2017. http://www.glamourmagazine.co.uk/gallery/gal-gadot-interview-face-of-gucci-bamboo-fragrance

Beaumont, Mark. "Get to Know Gal Gadot: The Wonder Woman 2017 Needs." *NME*, June 2, 2017. http://www.nme.com/features/gal-gadot-interview-woman-woman-2017-2082497#Gl5blkk8b57l5suE.99

DeGeneres, Ellen. "The 'Wonder'ful Gal Gadot." *The Ellen Show*, March 15, 2016. https://www.youtube.com/watch?v=NTySVAtrdQc

"*Fast & Furious 6* Star Gal Gadot Beauty Interview." *Real Style Network*, May 2013. http://www.realstylenetwork.com/beauty/2013/05/fast-furious-6-star-gal-gadot-beauty-interview/

"Film Interview: Gal Gadot." *Bring the Noise*, September 2013. http://www.bringthenoiseuk.com/201309/music/interviews/film-interview-gal-gadot-gisele-fast-furious-6

"Gal Gadot Is Wonder Woman: 'She Is Not Relying on a Man, and She's Not There Because of a Love Story.'" *Glamour*. March 7, 2016. https://www.glamour.com/story/gal-gadot-wonder-woman-cover-interview

Glock, Allison. "The Conversation: Actor, Mother, and Superhero Gal Gadot." ESPN, May 30, 2017. http://www.espn.com/espnw/culture/article/19496814/actor-mother-superhero-gal-gadot

Glock, Allison. "No Small Wonder: Gal Gadot Takes Summer by Storm." *Marie Claire*, May 8, 2017. http://www.marieclaire.com/celebrity/a26979/gal-gadot-june-2017-cover/

Hirschberg, Lynn. "Gal Gadot Listened to Beyoncé to Prepare for Her Wonder Woman Audition." *W Magazine*, April 12, 2017. https://www.wmagazine.com/story/gal-gadot-wonder-woman-beyonce

Jacobs, Laura. "Meet Gal Gadot, Our New Wonder Woman." *Vanity Fair*, July 10, 2015. https://www.vanityfair.com/hollywood/2015/07/gal-galdot-wonder-woman-miss-israel

McNeice, Mia. "How Serving in the Israeli Army Helped Prepare *Batman v. Superman*'s Gal Gadot to Play Wonder Woman." *People*, March 31, 2016. http://people.com/movies/how-serving-in-the-israeli-army-helped-prepare-gal-gadot-for-wonder-woman/

O'Neill, Carolina. "Meet Your Newest Wonder Woman, Gal Gadot." *Marie Claire*, August 24, 2015. http://www.marieclaire.com/celebrity/news/g3125/wonder-woman-gal-gadot/?slide=(2 and 3)

Sperling, Nicole. "Gal Gadot Did Reshoots for Wonder Woman While Pregnant." *Entertainment Weekly*, April 25, 2017. http://ew.com/movies/2017/04/25/gal-gadot-wonder-woman-reshoots-pregnant/

Truong, Peggy. "10 Things to Know about *Wonder Woman*'s Gal Gadot." *Cosmopolitan*, June 6, 2017. http://www.cosmopolitan.com/entertainment/celebs/a9868643/gal-gadot-wonder-woman-facts/

On the Internet

Ducksters: "Wonder Woman"
https://www.ducksters.com/biography/wonder_woman.php

Superhero Universe: "Wonder Woman"
http://superherouniverse.com/superheroes/wonderwoman.htm

adrenaline (uh-DREH-nuh-lin)—A chemical the body produces when a person is in danger or under stress; it speeds up the heart and breathing.

audition (aw-DIH-shun)—A test, usually in the form of a performance.

chakra (CHAH-kruh)—According to some beliefs, any of the power centers in the body.

choreographer (kor-ee-AH-gruh-fer)—The person who plans and designs a dance or other event that involves movement.

confidential (kon-fih-DEN-shul)—Secret; not to be shared with the public.

contestant (kun-TES-tunt)—A player in a game or contest.

gauntlet (GONT-let)—A series of difficult challenges.

lasso (LAS-oh)—A rope tied so that it can be thrown around a horse, cow, or criminal.

logistics (loh-JIS-tiks)—The handling of complicated details.

pageant (PAD-jent)—A colorful show or contest.

Shabbat (shah-BAHT)—The sabbath, or holy day, in Judaism. It is celebrated each week from sundown on Friday until sundown on Saturday.